A Cosmic Adventure Praising God!

Music

MW00964986

Contents

Note: Leaders working with preschoolers and kindergartners should refer to the *Preschool/Kindergarten Director* resource for complete instructions. If you are working with children with special needs, please consult *GALACTIC BLAST for Children With Special Needs*, available as a download from www.cokesburyvbs.com.

A Cosmic Adventure Praising God!

Day	Bible Story	Praise Phrase	Bible Booster	Discovery Time
Session 1 Mission: Creation of the Universe	**Genesis 1:1–2:4** Space Connection: **Earth**	**Our God is wonderful! Praise God!** Color of the day: **Green**	The earth is the LORD's and all that is in it, the world, and those who live in it. (Psalm 24:1, NRSV)	★ And Then There Was Light ★ Perfect Motion ★ Gravity Grabs
Session 2 Mission: Elijah at Mt. Horeb	**1 Kings 19:4-18** Space Connection: **Moon**	**Our God is incredible! Praise God!** Color of the day: **Red**	But for me it is good to be near God. (Psalm 73:28a, NRSV)	★ Listening ★ Seeing and Knowing
Session 3 Mission: The Woman at the Well	**John 4:1-42** Space Connection: **Stars**	**Our God is amazing! Praise God!** Color of the day: **Blue**	O LORD, you have searched me and known me. (Psalm 139:1, NRSV)	★ Daytime Starlight ★ Nighttime Starlight ★ Twinkling Stars
Session 4 Mission: A Blind Beggar in Jericho	**Luke 18:35-43** Space Connection: **Comet**	**Our God is magnificent! Praise God!** Color of the day: **Yellow**	The voice of the LORD is powerful; the voice of the LORD is full of majesty. (Psalm 29:4, NRSV)	★ Beggar Is Not a Pushover ★ What Do You See?
Session 5 Mission: Two Disciples in Emmaus	**Luke 24:13-32** Space Connection: **Supernova**	**Our God is awesome! Praise God!** Color of the day: **Purple**	The LORD lives! Praise be to my Rock! Exalted be God my Savior! (Psalm 18:46, NIV)	★ Light Tag ★ Excitement Explosion

Snack	Mission	Crafts	Recreation	Music
★ **Galactic Praise Snackers** **Easy Snacks** ★ String Cheese Shuttles ★ Cosmic Candy **Healthy Snack** ★ Fruit Cocktail Fuel	**Katie's Garden** (Katie Stagliano)	★ Galactic Sand Art (all ages) ★ Creation Wall Hanging & Quilt (elementary/tween) ★ Planet Earth Tissue Creation (preschool)	★ Creation Station Relay ★ Planet Toss ★ Guess God's Wonders	★ "Galactic Blast" ★ "Praise God" ★ "It's Wonderful"
★ **Near Me Moon Cakes** **Easy Snacks** ★ Over-the-Moon Pies ★ Moonbeam Muffins **Healthy Snack** ★ Lunar Bagels	**Ashlee's Toy Closet** (Ashlee Smith)	★ Moonbeam Tambourine (all ages) ★ Praise God Canvas Art (all ages)	★ Stick to It! ★ Whisper on the Mountain ★ Hear Me, Elijah!	★ "You and Me Together" ★ "Revolution" ★ "Fill Me With Praises"
★ **Amazing Space Mix** **Easy Snacks** ★ Amazing Space Mix II ★ Jacob's Well Dips **Healthy Snack** ★ Constellation Club Sandwiches	**Maxwell's Birthday Wish** (Maxwell Lawson)	★ Spectacular Star Clappers (all ages) ★ Constellation Magnets (elementary/tween) ★ Sparkling Stars (preschool)	★ Star Snatch ★ Living Water Fill-Up ★ Memory Booster	★ "A-M-A-Z-I-N-G" ★ "A New Life in Me"
★ **Comet Coolers** **Easy Snacks** ★ Jericho Juicers ★ Magnificent Praise Pops **Healthy Snack** ★ Starship Smoothie	**A Nickelby Difference** (Nicholas Marriam and Shelby McKnew)	★ God Cares Comet Frame (all ages) ★ Cosmic Craft Photo Frame (all ages) ★ Cosmic Craft Memory Page (all ages)	★ See Again! ★ Melt the Comet ★ Who Is It?	★ "God of Wonders" ★ "Let Everything That Has Breath"
★ **Supernova Sundaes** **Easy Snacks** ★ Intergalactic Ice Cream Cups ★ Space Cadet Ice Cream **Healthy Snack** ★ Go Galactic Yogurt	**Kennedy Cares** (Kennedy Jet Kulish)	★ Praise Supernova (all ages) ★ Solar Bead Cross Necklace (elementary/tween) ★ Cosmic Craft Stencils (preschool)	★ Awesome Stepping ★ Supernova Explosion ★ Old To New	★ Sing your favorites!

Planning Music for Your Cadets

Becoming familiar with the music is the first step in preparing to lead your cadets.

★ Listen to the *Complete Music CD* and read through the hand and body motions suggested in this guide.

★ Connect the words and phrases to the movements for each song.

★ Look for the movements and lyrics for the songs on the *Music Video DVD*.

Schedule

Some of the songs relate specifically to certain sessions; others are more general and theme related. The following is a suggested schedule for which songs should be taught in which sessions.

Session One

"Galactic Blast"

This high-energy theme song launches your cadets' VBS experience! Introduce each day at GALACTIC BLAST with this song, and get your cadets pumped and ready for their cosmic adventures!

"Praise God"

This simple but fun song teaches the five Praise Phrases your cadets will learn over the course of VBS. One test church had great success singing the chorus as a call-and-response between two groups of children or between leaders and children.

"It's Wonderful"

A reflection on the Session One Bible story, this song captures the sense of wonder we feel when we ponder God's creation.

Session Two

"You and Me Together"

This groovin' tune reminds cadets of the joy found in a close relationship with God, echoing the key teaching from the Session Two Bible story.

"Revolution"

A test church favorite, "Revolution" is a high-powered pop hit that celebrates God's presence and endless love.

"Fill Me With Praises"

Perfect for transitioning into quiet moments, this prayerful melody reinforces the concept of praising God.

Session Three

"A-M-A-Z-I-N-G"

Building on Session Three's Bible story and Praise Phrase, this test-church favorite spells out just how amazing God is!

"A New Life in Me"

Sessions Three, Four, and Five all feature Bible characters whose lives were changed by encounters with Jesus. Cadets singing this song will discover that Jesus offers them a new life, too.

Session Four

"God of Wonders"

This familiar worship song offers praise to the Lord of all creation and Creator of all the galaxy's wonders.

"Let Everything That Has Breath"

This popular praise song was a natural choice for this year's music program as the chorus teaches the overarching Bible verse (Psalm 150:6).

Session Five

Teaching all of the songs prior to the last session lets you sing your favorites on the final day. The two songs that fit best with the last session's message are "Praise God" and "A New Life in Me."

Music Correlation Chart

Use the chart below to find resources to help you teach all of the music at GALACTIC BLAST.

Song Title	Lyrics and Body Motions	Sheet Music	Complete Music CD: full track	Complete Music CD: instrumental only	Complete Music CD: PowerPoint slide
Galactic Blast	Page 7	Page 18	Track #1	Track #11	Slide #1
Revolution	Pages 8–9	Page 22	Track #2	Track #12	Slide #7
God of Wonders	Page 10	Page 27	Track #3	Track #13	Slide #16
A-M-A-Z-I-N-G	Page 11	Page 32	Track #4	Track #14	Slide #22
A New Life in Me	Page 12	Page 36	Track #5	Track #15	Slide #28
Let Everything That Has Breath	Page 13	Page 41	Track #6	Track #16	Slide #34
It's Wonderful	Page 14	Page 47	Track #7	Track #17	Slide #41
You and Me Together	Page 15	Page 51	Track #8	Track #18	Slide #49
Praise God	Page 16	Page 55	Track #9	Track #19	Slide #55
Fill Me With Praises	Page 17	Page 59	Track #10	Track #20	Slide #60

In addition:
★ The *Music Video DVD* features cadets just like yours demonstrating the hand and body movements for all ten songs.
★ The *Student Take-Home CD-ROM* makes all ten songs available to your cadets so they can listen to their favorites long after VBS.
★ **New this year!** Full tracks for all ten songs can be downloaded at www.cokesburyvbs.com. Purchase individual tracks or the whole album!

Decorating Ideas for Moons & Tunes

Resources

☆ *Activity Center Sign*, "Moons & Tunes"
☆ *Decorating Transparencies*, "Space Items I"
☆ *Music Leader*
☆ *Complete Music CD*
☆ *Music Video DVD*

Materials

☆ white mini lights
☆ white butcher paper
☆ paint (gray, green, blue, brown, and white)
☆ boxes or crates
☆ eggshell mattress pad
☆ battery-powered riding toy
☆ silver disco ball
☆ black plastic sheeting
☆ CD player
☆ TV and DVD player
☆ computer, projector, and projection screen, or posterboard and markers (optional)

Decorating Tips

★ Hang the "Moons & Tunes" *Activity Center Sign* in a prominent place by the doorway.

★ Create a space for a stage area where the music leader can easily be seen by all of the children when they are standing, singing, and doing the motions. String white mini lights over this area.

★ To create the appearance of a lunar surface, brush streaks of gray paint in a random pattern onto white butcher paper; crinkle the paper and use it to line the perimeter of the room and the stage area. Shape the paper over boxes or crates to make large moon rocks.

★ Add a few bootprints cut from an eggshell mattress pad to look like footprints on the moon. Place a battery-powered riding toy in one corner to look like a lunar rover. Hang a disco ball from the ceiling to give the sense of starlight.

★ Astronauts standing on the moon have an amazing view of Earth. To capture this panorama, cover one wall with black plastic sheeting and paint a large Earth on it.

★ Plug in the CD player and cue the *Complete Music CD*. Put the television where it is visible to everyone and cue the *Music Video DVD*. Alternatively, display the lyrics on a projection screen or write them on posterboard and hang on the walls.

Photo: Matt Huesmann

Galactic Blast

Lyrics	Motions
10, 9, 8, 7, 6, 5　4-3-2-1!	*Punch alternating fists over head for each number*
Blast off! Here we go,	*Jump up, arms straight over head*
racin' through space, rockin' round the globe!	*Step in place, swinging arms from side to side*
Fly by galaxies; see God's world like it's in 3-D!	*Hold arms to sides like airplane wings and pretend to fly*
We got our mission,	*Salute with R hand*
a lifetime plan,	*Extend R arm to side and lower*
a cosmic adventure, a holy command.	*Make twinkling stars over head by opening and closing fists, alternating R and L hands*
Give God the glory for all we see,	*Sign for "glory": Clap R hand to L, then make an arc with the R hand, hand shaking*
Creator of everything, A to Z!	*Extend arms to the front and open to sides*

Chorus

Lyrics	Motions
Blast off	*Jump up, arms straight over head*
like a rocket ship.	*Circle R arm back*
Set our praises a blazin'!	*Circle L arm back*
Blast off!	*Jump up, arms straight over head*
It's a Good News trip.	*Circle R arm back*
Show our faith is amazin'!	*Circle L arm back*
Shout to heaven; joy and praise	*Put hands by mouth, palms facing out*
to the very last star and past.	*Reach R arm to left over head, then draw it in an arc to the right, like a shooting star*
Let's go	*Jump up, arms straight over head*
on a Galactic Blast!	*Wave arms from side to side, starting right*

Lyrics	Motions
Jump in the air	*Jump to the right; bounce knees once*
like you're launchin' to space. (Ho-oh)	*Jump to the left; bounce knees once*
Shake your hands high in a cosmic praise. (Hey-ey)	*Wave arms right-left-right; left-right-left*
Turn a circle in a orbit of love. (Wo-oh)	*Walk in a circle to the right, arms extended to sides*
Blast "Praise the Lord!" to the	*Put hands by mouth, palms facing out*
heavens above!	*Point to sky three times*

Repeat chorus through "very last star and past."

Lyrics	Motions
Let's go	*Jump up, arms straight over head*
on a trip galactic—	*Wave arms right-left-right*
let's go	*Jump up, arms straight over head*
where it's all fantastic—	*Wave arms left-right-left*
let's go	*Jump up, arms straight over head*
on a Galactic Blast!	*Wave arms from side to side, starting right*

WORDS: Matt Huesmann
MUSIC: Matt Huesmann
© 2009 Matt Huesmann/ASCAP

Revolution

Let's go	With palms facing each other, place hands on either side of face
hyperspace	Rotate hands so R hand is over head and L hand is under chin; palms face down
on a mission	With palms facing each other, place hands on either side of face
to seek your face,	Rotate hands so L hand is over head and R hand is under chin; palms face down
each day	Shoot R arm up, palm facing up
closer to you.	Lower R arm
You're all that I need,	Punch R-L-R-R over head, hands in fists
love and peace, at light speed.	Punch L-R-L-L over head, hands in fists
Every good	Shoot R arm up, palm facing up
thing comes from you.	Lower R arm
Lord, take my heart; I wanna be	Press palms over heart, then extend arms
surprised,	Put hands in fists by eyes, then open fingers
live my life through your	Sign for "life": use index fingers and thumbs of both hands to make L shapes, with index fingers pointing toward each other; start at waist and draw up body
eyes.	Point to eyes
Be the heart, the soul, the center of me.	Circle arms toward center of the body, up, out to sides
Chorus	
Oh, you orbit my world	Jump three times in a circle to the right
in an endless revolution.	Jump three times in a circle to the left
You're my	Kick R foot forward and extend arms forward, wrists crossed
gravity,	Bend knees, hands on thighs
my strength and my solution,	Face slightly R; make a football goal with hands in fists
there with me,	Roll fists in a circle
from the start	Extend arms, hands clasped
to the conclusion.	Bring clasped hands in front of chest
I'm	Point to self with thumbs
surrounded by love,	Press hands over heart, at the same time swinging chest down and to the left; pivot to face front
in an endless revolution.	Jump three times in a circle to the right
Up,	Shoot arms over head
down,	Put hands on hips
round and round,	Circle head twice
like a circle, in surround,	Bounce hips in a circle
your voice	Shoot R arm up, palm facing up
is callin' to me.	Lower R arm
Live in every part,	Punch R-L-R-R over head, hands in fists
every beat of my heart.	Punch L-R-L-L over head, hands in fists
I need you	Shoot R arm up, palm facing up
always with me.	Lower R arm

WORDS: Matt Huesmann
MUSIC: Matt Huesmann
© 2009 Matt Huesmann/ASCAP

Lord, take my heart; I wanna be
surprised.
Live my life through your
eyes.
Be the heart, the soul, the center of me.

Repeat chorus

Round and round, round my heart you go,

round and round, round my heart you go,
round and round, round my heart you go,
round and around and around and around—

Repeat chorus

Press palms over heart, then extend arms
Put hands in fists by eyes, then open fingers
Sign for "life"
Point to eyes
Circle arms toward center of the body, up, out to sides

"Orbit" three times—twice fast, once slow (see description below)
"Orbit" three times—twice fast, once slow
"Orbit" three times—twice fast, once slow
"Orbit" four times—three times fast, once very slow

Orbit: This move is often known as the "Cabbage Patch." With hands in fists, extend arms to the left side. Circle the arms clockwise to the right side, then bend elbows as the fists approach the chest. Continue in a clockwise "orbit."

God of Wonders

Lord of all creation,

of water, earth, and sky,
the heavens are Your tabernacle.
Glory to the Lord on high.

Chorus
God of wonders, beyond our galaxy,
You are holy, holy.
The universe declares Your majesty.
You are holy, holy.
Lord of heaven
and earth.
Lord of heaven
and earth.

Early in the morning

I will celebrate the light.
When I stumble in the darkness
I will call Your name by night.

Repeat chorus

Hallelujah
to the Lord of heaven
and earth.
Hallelujah
to the Lord of heaven
and earth.
Hallelujah
to the Lord of heaven
and earth.

Repeat chorus

Lord of heaven
and earth.

Sign for "Lord": move R hand in L-position from L shoulder to R waist
Extend arms down, forward, and up
Sway with arms in V over head
Sign for "glory": Clap R hand to L, then make an arc with the R hand, hand shaking

With R hand, draw an arc over head from left to right
Press palms together in prayer
With L hand, draw an arc over head from right to left
Press palms together in prayer
Sign for "Lord"
Unfold arms forward, palms facing up and elbows bent
Sign for "Lord"
Unfold arms forward, palms facing up and elbows bent

Put hands in fists in front of chest, L elbow up and R elbow down; arch back as if stretching
Open hands and move them away from each other
Round forward, hands in fists
Open arms, elbows bent, palms up

Shake hands on either side of face
Sign for "Lord"
Unfold arms forward, palms facing up and elbows bent
Shake hands on either side of face
Sign for "Lord"
Unfold arms forward, palms facing up and elbows bent
Shake hands on either side of face
Sign for "Lord"
Unfold arms forward, palms facing up and elbows bent

Sign for "Lord"
Unfold arms forward, palms facing up and elbows bent

WORDS: Marc Byrd and Steve Hindalong
MUSIC: Marc Byrd and Steve Hindalong
© 2000 New Spring Publishing, Inc. / Never Say Never Songs (ASCAP) (Administered by Brentwood-Benson Music Publishing, Inc.)
Storm Boy Music / (BMI) / Meaux Mercy (Admin. EMI Christian Music Group)

A-M-A-Z-I-N-G

Lyrics	Motions
A woman at a well one day	*Walk in place, elbows bent, palms facing up*
met a stranger on her way.	*Walk in place, elbows bent, palms facing up*
All his words left her simply	*Raise hands in fists next to eyes*
amazed.	*Open hands with fingers spread*
Jesus said, "New life I give.	*Sign for "Jesus": touch R middle finger to L palm; touch L middle finger to R palm*
I have what you need to live.	*Sign for "live": use index fingers and thumbs of both hands to make L shapes, with index fingers pointing toward each other; start at waist and draw up body*
I'm with you now and always." (Oh)	*Open arms to front, elbows bent, palms up*

Chorus

A-M-A-Z-I-N-G—	*Wave R arm, palm flat, in the air left-right-left-right*
that's your love for me.	*Bend knees and bounce four times while pulsing bent arms upward at hip level*
A-M-A-Z-I-N-G—	*Wave L arm, palm flat, in the air right-left-right-left*
how you care for me.	*Bend knees and bounce four times while pulsing bent arms upward at hip level*
A-M-A-Z-I-N-G—	*Wave R arm, palm flat, in the air left-right-left-right*
what you see in me.	*Bend knees and bounce four times while pulsing bent arms upward at hip level*
Love beyond all my wrongs,	*Press palms over heart*
you died and set me free.	*Sign for "free": With index fingers pressed to thumbs to make a circle, cross hands at wrists, palms facing in; uncross hands, palms facing out*
A-M-A-Z-I-N-G—	*Wave L arm, palm flat, in the air right-left-right-left-right-left-right*
my God's	*Shoot both arms out to sides*
amazing!	*Cross arms over chest to hug self*

Lord, you know me inside out,	*Walk in place, elbows bent, palms facing up*
all my thoughts, my fears and doubts,	*Walk in place, elbows bent, palms facing up*
when my faith is really put to test.	*Raise hands in fists in front of eyes*
I might stumble, I might fall.	*Round forward, hands in fists*
You walk with me through it all.	*Stand up straight and march in place*
You're always with me. I'm blessed! (Oh!)	*Open arms to front, elbows bent, palms up*

Repeat chorus

Your grace is amazing!	*Grapevine right (step R to right, step L behind R, step R to right, tap L in place)*
	Three steps (L, R, L) turning to the left; clap
Your peace is amazing!	*Grapevine right*
	Three steps (L, R, L) turning to the left; clap
Your love is amazing!	*Grapevine right*
	Three steps (L, R, L) turning to the left; clap
A-M-A-Z-I-N-G—	*Wave R arm right-left-right-left-right-left-right, going a little lower each time*
amazing!	*Jump, landing with feet apart and arms in V over head*

Repeat chorus

WORDS: Matt Huesmann   MUSIC: Matt Huesmann   © 2009 Matt Huesmann/ASCAP

A New Life in Me

Like a star who's lost its light,
I was fading in the night,
wondering if someone even cared.

Then I heard a good friend say,
"Let Jesus change your life today.

He's waiting. Come to him in prayer."

Chorus
Now I got a new life

in me.
I got a life eternally.
I got a life of hope because of
Jesus'
love.
I got a new life
in me.
You rose from death to set me free.

I got a new life, a new life
in me.

What was bad
you changed to good,
saved my heart and made it new.
I'm walking every day with you.

You forgive me when I'm wrong,
with love unchanging, always strong.
I'm watching my life be renewed.

Repeat chorus

Repeat chorus to "set me free"

I got a new life,
a new life,
a new life,
a new life,
a new life,
a new life
in me.

Shoot R arm up, palm facing up
Lower R arm
Hold arms to sides, elbows raised, palms up

Hold R hand to R ear as if listening
Sign for "Jesus": touch R middle finger to L palm; touch L middle finger to R palm
Press palms together in prayer

Sign for "life": use index fingers and thumbs of both hands to make L shapes, with index fingers pointing toward each other; start at waist and draw up body
Point to self with thumbs
Extend arms forward, elbows bent, palms up
Sign for "life"
Sign for "Jesus"
Press palms over heart
Sign for "life"
Point to self with thumbs
Sign for "free": With index fingers pressed to thumbs to make a circle, cross hands at wrists, palms facing in; uncross hands, palms facing out
Sign for "life"
Point to self with thumbs

Give a double thumbs down
Give a double thumbs up
Use index fingers to draw a heart over chest
March in place

Sign for "forgive": stroke L palm with R fingers
Press palms over heart
Open arms to front, elbows bent, palms up

Sign for "life"
Raise R arm to right over head, hand open
Raise L arm to left over head, hand open
Lower R arm to right, hand open
Lower L arm to left, hand open
Sign for "life"
Point to self with thumbs

WORDS: Matt Huesmann
MUSIC: Matt Huesmann
© 2009 Matt Huesmann/ASCAP

Galactic Blast: A Cosmic Adventure Praising God!

Let Everything That Has Breath

Chorus
Let everything that, everything that, everything that
has breath praise the Lord.
Let everything that, everything that, everything that
has breath praise the Lord.

Slowly raise arms to V over head while bouncing knees
Punch both arms, hands in fists, over head five times
Slowly raise arms to V over head while bouncing knees
Punch both arms, hands in fists, over head five times

Praise You in the morning,
praise You in the evening,
praise You when I'm young
and when I'm old.
praise You when I'm laughing,
praise You when I'm grieving,
praise You every season
of the soul.

Raise both arms over head to right, hands shaking
Raise both arms over head to left, hands shaking
Raise both arms straight over head, hands shaking
Lower arms to sides, hands shaking
Raise both arms over head to right, hands shaking
Raise both arms over head to left, hands shaking
Raise both arms straight over head, hands shaking
Lower arms to sides, hands shaking

If we could see how much You're worth,
Your power, Your might,
Your endless love,
then surely we would never cease to praise.

Hold arms to sides, elbows raised, palms up
Raise R fist, then L fist, to make football goal
Press palms over heart
Extend arms to front and open to sides

Repeat chorus

Praise You in the heavens,
joining with the angels,
praising You forever
and a day.
Praise You on the earth now,
joining with creation,
calling all the nations
to Your praise.

Raise both arms over head to right, hands shaking
Raise both arms over head to left, hands shaking
Raise both arms straight over head, hands shaking
Lower arms to sides, hands shaking
Raise both arms over head to right, hands shaking
Raise both arms over head to left, hands shaking
Raise both arms straight over head, hands shaking
Lower arms to sides, hands shaking

If they could see how much You're worth,
Your power, Your might,
Your endless love,
then surely they would never cease to praise.

Hold arms to sides, elbows raised, palms up
Raise R fist, then L fist, to make football goal
Press palms over heart
Extend arms to front and open to sides

Repeat chorus three times

Everything that
has breath praise the Lord.

Raise arms to V over head
Punch both arms, hands in fists, over head five times

WORDS: Matt Redman
MUSIC: Matt Redman
© 1999 Thankyou Music

It's Wonderful

Lyrics	Motions
Lookin' up, sun in my face,	Place hands, palms up, on either side of head; look up
I'm simply mesmerized.	In same position, look from side to side
Birds soar high,	Point in an arc with R arm
clouds float on by,	Point in an arc with L arm
the wind blows through the sky.	Point in an arc with R arm
I'm not sure how you do it,	Hold arms to sides, elbows raised, palms up
but I love to watch and see.	Shield eyes with hands; look from side to side
The earth reflects your beauty,	Hands draw arcs in the air to form globe
your power and mystery.	Raise arms to make a football goal, hands in fists

Chorus

It's wonderful, it's marvelous,	Walk in a circle to right, arms extended to sides
the way we live and breathe.	Sign for "life": use index fingers and thumbs of both hands to make L shapes, with index fingers pointing toward each other; start at waist and draw up body

It's wonderful, to see God's hand	Walk in a circle to right, arms extended to sides
in all we touch and see.	Extend arms to front and open to sides
And it's like a glimpse of heaven, a peek at majesty.	Slowly raise arms from sides to V over head
Lord, you're so amazing and wonderful	Walk in a circle to right, arms extended to sides
to me.	Press palms over heart

Countless stars	Open R hand over head; open L hand over head
and endless sand,	Open R hand by hip; open L hand by hip
and still you know my name.	Point to self with thumbs
In my joy,	Press R palm over heart
through all my fears,	Press L palm on top over R palm over heart
you love me just the same.	Press both palms over heart
From mountaintops to valleys,	Make a mountain peak with fingertips in front of chest
every corner of the globe,	Hands draw arcs in the air to form globe
you watch and care for all things.	Shield eyes with hands; look from side to side
You love us and it shows.	Press palms over heart

Repeat chorus

Wonderful,	Swoop R arm in an arc from left to right over head
wonderful,	Swoop L arm in an arc from right to left over head
wonderful to me.	Swoop R arm in an arc from left to right over head
Wonderful,	Swoop L arm in an arc from right to left over head
wonderful,	Swoop R arm in an arc from left to right over head
so wonderful to me.	Swoop L arm in an arc from right to left over head

Repeat chorus

WORDS: Matt Huesmann
MUSIC: Matt Huesmann
© 2009 Matt Huesmann/ASCAP

You and Me Together

You're the best part of each day.	*Facing slightly R, point with both index fingers to sky*
Ya change my heart from night to day.	*Facing slightly L, point with both index fingers to sky*
Ya show me that your word is true.	*Facing forward, point with both index fingers to sky*
All the smiles and joy you see,	*Point to smile*
Lord, you put them all in me.	*Open arms to the front, elbows bent, palms up*
Chorus	
You	*Facing slightly R, point with both index fingers to sky*
and me together.	*Point to self with thumbs*
You	*Facing slightly L, point with both index fingers to sky*
and me forever.	*Point to self with thumbs*
Everywhere you lead I'll follow you.	*Extend R arm forward and walk in circle to right*
You tell me I'm worth it.	*Facing slightly R, give a double thumbs up*
I know you are perfect.	*Facing slightly L, give a double thumbs up*
Together, forever,	*Clasp hands in front of chest*
that's you	*Point to sky with both index fingers*
and me.	*Point to self with thumbs*
Like a full moon bright at night,	*Facing slightly R, point with both index fingers to sky*
you fill my darkness with your light.	*Facing slightly L, point with both index fingers to sky*
Ya show me that you're always there.	*Facing forward, point with both index fingers to sky*
If there's one thing I should do,	*Hold up R index finger, R arm extended forward*
Lord, it's give my life to you.	*Open arms to the front, elbows bent, palms up*
Repeat chorus	
You made	*Open R arm to side, elbow raised, palm up*
and you save.	*Open L arm to side, elbow raised, palm up*
You live	*Open R arm to front, elbow bent, palm up*
and you give.	*Open L arm to front, elbow bent, palm up*
Every day, every way,	*Raise arms in V over head*
you're always there	*Point to sky with both index fingers*
for me.	*Point to self with thumbs*
Repeat chorus to "perfect"	
Together, wherever,	*Clasp hands in front of chest*
forever and ever,	*Extend arms in front, hands clasped*
together, forever,	*Bring arms back into chest, hands clasped*
that's me	*Point to self with thumbs*
and you.	*Point to sky with both index fingers*

WORDS: Matt Huesmann
MUSIC: Matt Huesmann
© 2009 Matt Huesmann/ASCAP

Praise God

It's time to rise up, get off your seat.
Time to stand up, get on your feet.
It's a call: Every boy, every girl,

shout a Praise Phrase out to the world! Come on!

Slowly raise arms from sides to chest level
Slowly raise arms from chest level to V over head
Extend R arm across body, pointing to left; sweep arm across from left to right
Put open hands on either side of mouth

Chorus
Our God is wonderful!
Praise God!
Our God's incredible!
Praise God!
Our God is oh so
amazing!
Praise God!
Our God's magnificent!
Praise God!
Our God is awesome!
Praise God!
Worship and praise God's holy name.

Pump hands (palms flat) over head to right three times
Clap twice
Pump hands (palms flat) over head to left three times
Clap twice
Pump hands (palms flat) directly over head three times
Lower arms to side, shaking hands
Clap twice
Pump hands (palms flat) over head to right three times
Clap twice
Pump hands (palms flat) over head to left three times
Clap twice
Slowly raise arms to V over head

Repeat chorus

Worship and praise God's holy name.

Slowly raise arms to V over head

WORDS: Matt Huesmann
MUSIC: Matt Huesmann
© 2009 Matt Huesmann/ASCAP

Fill Me With Praises

You are my Maker, my God and Creator,

the breath of life that lives in me.
You bring compassion, you're hope everlasting,
and life that's eternally.

Chorus
Fill me
with praises.
Righteous and holy's your name.
Fill me
with praises.
You're always, forever, the same.
Fill me
with praises.
Each morning your mercies are new.
Fill me
with praises.
Lord of my life,

I love you.

I come to you weakened, tired,
and broken,

with nothing but my needy soul.
You're healing and mending; you're joy that's unending.
Your spirit of peace makes me whole.

Repeat chorus

Lord of my life,
I love you.

Sign for "God": with R hand open, palm facing left, make a shepherd's crook
Tap chest with R palm four times
Press palms over heart
Sign for "life": use index fingers and thumbs of both hands to make L shapes, with index fingers pointing toward each other; start at waist and draw up body

Press palms together in prayer
Open arms to V over head
Lower arms in front of body
Press palms together in prayer
Open arms to V over head
Lower arms in front of body
Press palms together in prayer
Open arms to V over head
Lower arms in front of body
Press palms together in prayer
Open arms to V over head
Sign for "Lord": move R hand in L-position from L shoulder to R waist
Press palms over heart

Press back of R hand to forehead, as if weary
Put hands in fists next to each other, then pull apart and down, as if breaking a stick
Open arms to the front, elbows bent and palms up
Pulse both palms over heart four times
Extend arms to front and open to sides

Sign for "Lord"
Press palms over heart

WORDS: Matt Huesmann
MUSIC: Matt Huesmann
© 2009 Matt Huesmann/ASCAP

Galactic Blast

(Theme Song)

WORDS: Matt Huesmann
MUSIC: Matt Huesmann
© 2009 Matt Huesmann/ASCAP

Galactic Blast: A Cosmic Adventure Praising God!

Revolution

A little funky! (♩ = 128)

Let's go hy - per-space on a mis - sion to seek your face, each day clos - er to you.

You're all that I need, love and peace, at light speed.

Ev - ery good thing comes from you. _____ Lord,

WORDS: Matt Huesmann
MUSIC: Matt Huesmann
© 2009 Matt Huesmann/ASCAP

start to the con-clu - sion. I'm sur-round-ed by love, __ in an end-less rev - o - lu -

tion. Up, down, round and round,

like a cir - cle, in sur-round, your voice is call-in' to me. __

Live in ev - ery part, ev - ery beat of my heart.

God of Wonders

WORDS: Marc Byrd and Steve Hindalong
MUSIC: Marc Byrd and Steve Hindalong
© 2000 New Spring Publishing, Inc. / Never Say Never Songs (ASCAP) (Administered by Brentwood-Benson Music Publishing, Inc.)
Storm Boy Music / (BMI) / Meaux Mercy (Admin. EMI Christian Music Group)

A-M-A-Z-I-N-G

1. A wo-man at ____ a well _ one day
(2. _) Lord, you know _ me in - side out,

met a stran - ger on __ her way. All his words _ left her _ sim - ply a-
all my thoughts, _ my fears _ and doubts, when my faith _ is real - ly put to

WORDS: Matt Huesmann
MUSIC: Matt Huesmann
© 2009 Matt Huesmann/ASCAP

A New Life in Me

WORDS: Matt Huesmann
MUSIC: Matt Huesmann
© 2009 Matt Huesmann/ASCAP

Galactic Blast: A Cosmic Adventure Praising God!

Galactic Blast: A Cosmic Adventure Praising God!

death to set __ me free. __   I got a   new   life, __   a

new   life, __   a new   life, __   a new   life, __   a

new   life, __   a new   life __ in   me. __

Let Everything That Has Breath

WORDS: Matt Redman
MUSIC: Matt Redman
© 1999 Thankyou Music

joined - ing _ with cre-a - tion, _ call-ing all the na-tions to Your praise. If

they could see how much You're worth, Your pow'r, Your might, Your end - less love, then

sure - ly they would nev - er cease to praise.

Let ev - 'ry - thing _ that, ev - 'ry - thing _ that, ev - 'ry - thing _ that

It's Wonderful

With feeling (♩ = 144)

1. Look - in' up, ___ ___ sun in my face, ___ I'm sim - ply mes - mer - ized. ___
2. Count - less stars ___ and end - less sand, ___ and still you know ___ my name. ___

___ Birds soar high, ___ ___ clouds float on by, ___ the
___ In my joy, ___ through all ___ my fears, ___ you

You and Me Together

Fun! (♩ = 85)

1. You're the best part of each day.
2. Like a full moon bright at night,

Praise God

Driving (♩ = 120)

It's time to rise up, get off your seat. Time to stand up,

get on your feet. It's a call: Ev-ery boy, ev-ery girl,—

WORDS: Matt Huesmann
MUSIC: Matt Huesmann
© 2009 Matt Huesmann/ASCAP

Galactic Blast: A Cosmic Adventure Praising God!

Fill Me With Praises

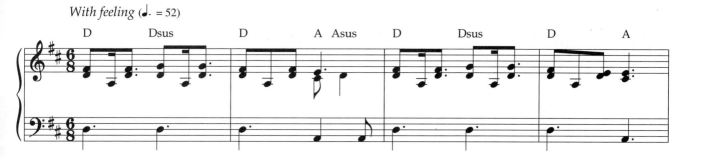

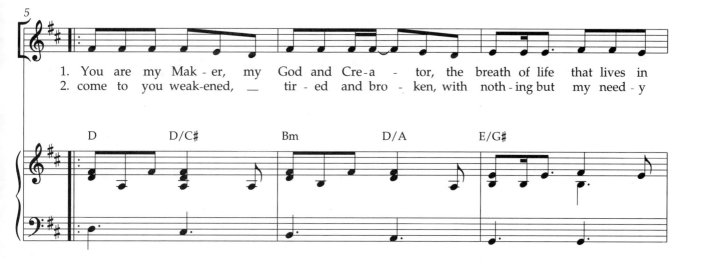

1. You are my Mak - er, my God and Cre-a - tor, the breath of life that lives in
2. come to you weak-ened, __ tir - ed and bro - ken, with noth - ing but my need - y

me. __ You bring com - pas - sion, you're hope ev - er - last - ing, and
soul. You're heal - ing and mend - ing, you're joy that's un - end - ing. Your

Music With Preschoolers

Use the following ideas if you are leading preschoolers in music time. Complete instructions for these activities are found in the *Preschool/Kindergarten Director.*

Preparation and Notes

★ Select the number of songs and activities you feel will best meet your needs for the time span.

★ Arrange with the preschool/kindergarten leader that the children will make maracas during their class time and bring them to music time. Alternatively, the maracas can be made as part of music time.

★ Play the GALACTIC BLAST music as children enter and exit music time. Select one, two, or all of these options to use today.

Today's Songs

★ "Galactic Blast"

★ "Praise God"

★ "It's Wonderful"

Say: **Our God is wonderful! Praise God!** Now ask them to say the Praise Phrase with you and shake their maracas to the beat.

Praising God's Universe

Using the script provided in the *Preschool/ Kindergarten Director* on page 32, tell the creation story. Show the children pictures of the items mentioned as you tell the story. Have the children respond with the Praise Phrase. Tell the story again while the children walk or march around the room, shaking their maracas.

GALACTIC BLAST Music

Use the maracas as rhythm instruments. Have the children shake them as they march around the room singing "Praise God."

Rhythm Activity

Have the children stand in a circle. Say: **To help us learn each other's names, we're going to stamp out the beats of our names. Let's find out whose names have a similar pattern! Let's stamp out the word Earth. One stamp. Now let's stamp out the word universe. Three stamps. It was a longer word, wasn't it? Some of our names will be long and some will be short.**

Go around the circle, giving everyone (including teachers) a chance to say their name and stamp out the syllables. Say: _____ **is here today. Praise God!**

Preparation and Notes

★ Select the number of songs and activities you feel will best meet your needs for the time span.

★ Arrange with the preschool/kindergarten leader that the children will make tambourines during their class time and bring them to music time. Alternatively, the tambourines can be made as part of music time.

★ Play GALACTIC BLAST music as children enter and exit music time.

Today's Songs

★ "Let Everything That Has Breath"

★ "You and Me Together"

★ "Fill Me With Praises"

Moon and Sun Are So Much Fun

Teach the poem and follow-up activity found on page 48 of the *Preschool/Kindergarten Director.*

GALACTIC BLAST Music

Use the tambourines as rhythm instruments. Have the children shake them as they march around the room singing "You and Me Together."

Rhythm Activity

Teach the words and the sign language for the overarching Bible verse, Psalm 150:6: "Let everything that breathes praise the LORD!"

Then sing the following lyrics to the tune of "If You're Happy and You Know It."

Speak the words "Praise God!" Clap when you say "Praise" and stomp when you say "God."

Let everything that breathes
praise the LORD!
Praise God!
Let everything that breathes
praise the LORD!
Praise God!
Let everything that breathes,
let everything that breathes,
let everything that breathes
praise the LORD!
Praise God!

Preparation and Notes

★ Select the number of songs and activities you feel will best meet your needs for the time span.

★ Arrange with the preschool/kindergarten leader that the children will make bell bracelets during their class time and bring them to music time. Alternatively, the bracelets can be made as part of music time.

★ Play the GALACTIC BLAST music as the children enter and exit music time.

Today's Songs

★ "A-M-A-Z-I-N-G"
★ "A New Life in Me"
★ "Praise God" or "Fill Me With Praises"

Five-Pointed Star

For a warm-up activity, have the kids make five-pointed stars with their bodies. Have them spread their feet apart, raise their arms to shoulder level, and smile. Count off the points: one is their head, two is their left arm, three is their right arm, four is their left foot, and five is their right foot. Congratulate them on making great stars.

Finger Play Star Activity

Teach the rhyme found on page 64 of the *Preschool/Kindergarten Director*.

Say the rhyme again and encourage the children to hold up the same number of fingers as you. When you get to the last line, let the children jump up and spread out their arms and legs wide to be a five-pointed star.

GALACTIC BLAST Music

Use the bell bracelets as rhythm instruments. Have the children shake them as they march around the room singing "Praise God" or "Fill Me With Praises."

Rhythm Activity

Photocopy a star pattern onto tagboard or posterboard. Cut out the star shapes and tape them to the floor. Make one star per child, plus several extra.

Tell the children they are going on a Star Search. While the music is playing, they can dance, walk, or move any way they want. When music stops and you say "Star Search!" children must jump or hop on one of the stars. Make sure everyone finds a star. Continue to play as time and interest allow.

Preparation and Notes

★ Select the number of songs and activities you feel will best meet your needs for the time span.

★ Arrange with the preschool/kindergarten leader that the children will make streamers during their class time and bring them to music time. Alternatively, the streamers can be made as part of music time.

★ Play the GALACTIC BLAST music as the children enter and exit music time.

Today's Songs

★ "God of Wonders"
★ "Revolution"
★ "Praise God" or "Fill Me With Praises"

GALACTIC BLAST Music

After the children make their streamers, say: **While we are at GALACTIC BLAST VBS, we're discovering ways to praise God. Let's use our praise streamers as we sing our songs praising God.**

Let's say today's Praise Phrase. Our God is magnificent! Praise God!

Rhythm Activity

Sing "Jump, Turn, Praise!" to the tune of "Pick a Bale of Cotton." The lyrics and motions can be found on page 80 of the *Preschool/Kindergarten Director*.

Preparation and Notes

★ Select the number of songs and activities you feel will best meet your needs for the time span.

★ Arrange with the preschool/kindergarten leader that the children will make egg shakers during their class time and bring them to music time. Alternatively, the shakers can be made as part of music time.

★ Play the GALACTIC BLAST music as the children enter and exit music time.

Today's Songs

★ "Praise God"

★ "Fill Me With Praises"

★ Sing your favorites from the week!

Praise Band

After the children are seated, say: **While we are at GALACTIC BLAST VBS, we're discovering ways to praise God. Let's use pots and pans to make a Praise Band!**

Hand out pot and pans. Show the children how to turn the items upside down and drum to the beat with their hands or with wooden spoons.

GALACTIC BLAST Music

Use the egg shakers as rhythm instruments. Have the children shake them as they march around the room singing "Praise God."

Rhythm Activity

Have a parade to celebrate that Jesus is alive. While the children are marching around the room, say: **Our God is awesome! Praise God! Jesus lives! Praise God!** Let children shake their egg shakers as they march.